115 85

At Deine's
CAMERA WORKSHOP

115 85

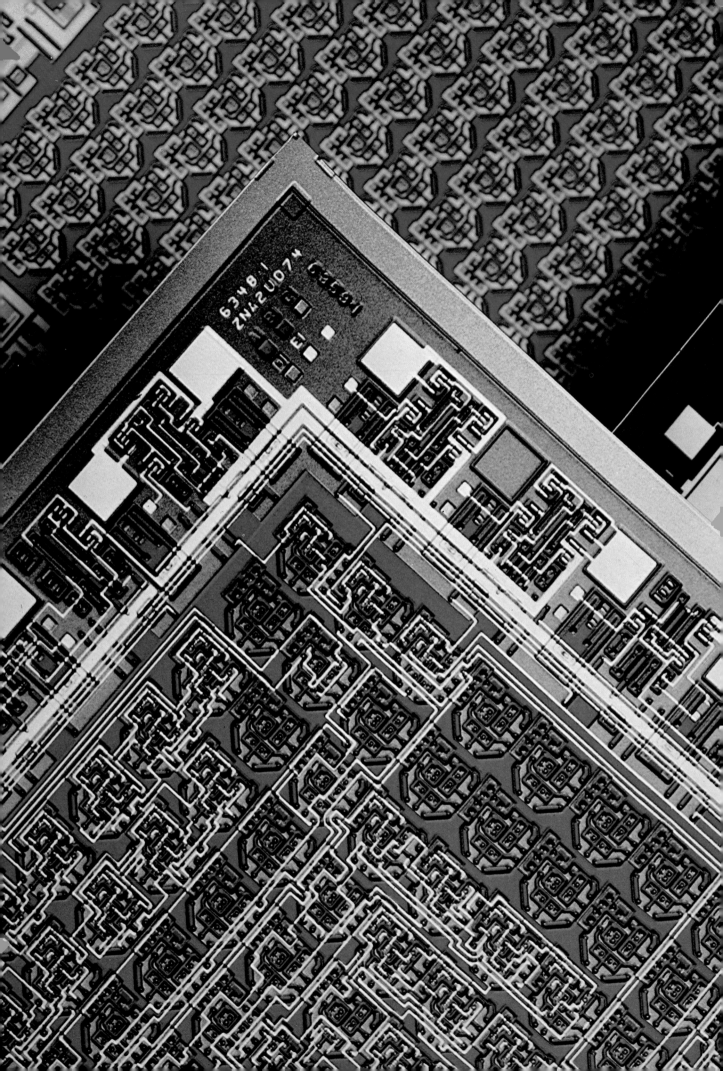

The author

Neil Ardley is the author of many books for both adults and children. Having obtained his degree in science, he worked in patents and in publishing before becoming a full-time writer. He is also well known for his work as a composer and performer of synthesizer music.

Previous pages

The future lies in microchips, which are miniature but complicated electrical devices that can handle information and make calculations in huge quantities at bewildering speeds. The microchip shown here is magnified about one thousand times and is seen in stages of its manufacture before and after connections are made to its many components. Microchips like this will affect all our lives in all kinds of ways as we forge ahead into the future.

WORLD OF TOMORROW

HEALTH AND MEDICINE

NEIL ARDLEY

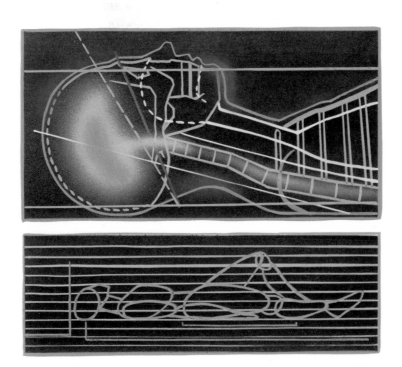

FRANKLIN WATTS
London · New York · Toronto · Sydney

Contents

Foreword   8
Caring for the future   10
Medicine before birth   12
Helping yourself   14
Tooth troubles   16
Computer doctor   18
The war against disease   20
Exploring the body   22
Emergency room   24
Hospital of the future   26
Spare-part medicine   28
Bionic people   30
Aiding the disabled   32
Conquering pain   34
Glossary   36
Index   37

© Franklin Watts Limited 1982

First published in Great Britain 1982
Franklin Watts Limited
8 Cork Street
London W1

First published in the USA by
Franklin Watts Inc.
387 Park Avenue South
New York, N.Y. 10016

UK edition: ISBN 0 85166 951 4
US edition: ISBN 0-531-04474-2
Library of Congress
Catalog Card No: 82-50060

Foreword

The future should bring many ways of improving our lives, but none so exciting as advances in medicine. As doctors and scientists gain more and more knowledge about the human body, they will find new ways to fight disease and conquer pain. The methods may take advantage of the processes by which the body defends itself, keeping us healthy in natural ways. No one should ever have to suffer prolonged pain or illness.

This family of the future is playing a game together. Everyone, young or old, is healthy and full of life, thanks to intensive medical attention. In the future, health care will begin even before birth and will continue throughout life. Computers will help doctors to watch over people, working to ensure that no one enters life with medical defects. They may also help to prevent any subsequent illness from developing.

9

Caring for the future

This scene shows a visit to the doctor in the future. However, the patient isn't there; in fact, he or she hasn't yet been born or even conceived. The people are ensuring the health of a person who is yet-to-be, for in the world of tomorrow medical care may begin long before you are born. The doctor and his visitors are also making certain that generations of people who will be born far in the future will lead healthy lives.

The man and woman have come to the doctor because they intend to have children. They want to make sure that their children will be as healthy as possible. The doctor can help them by studying their genes. He takes samples of their body cells and checks the genes inside the cells. Every cell in a person's body has the same kind of genes, which give a person their own particular features and characteristics. These may include certain medical conditions as well as a long nose or red hair, for example.

The doctor's computer is showing the genetic code of each of his visitors. This code is the arrangement of chemicals in their genes. Every person has his or her own particular genetic code which makes their genes different from everyone else's genes. The code is inherited from one's parents and is a mixture of their codes.

By comparing the genetic codes of the man and woman, the doctor can advise them what their children should be like. If the children are likely to inherit a genetic code that produces a defect or a medical condition, the doctor will be ready to provide treatment before birth to alter the code and give them healthy genes.

Most inherited illnesses, which include some mental disorders, are now impossible for doctors to cure. But with genetic advice, fewer and fewer children should be born with inherited defects. Some of the saddest human conditions could vanish for ever.

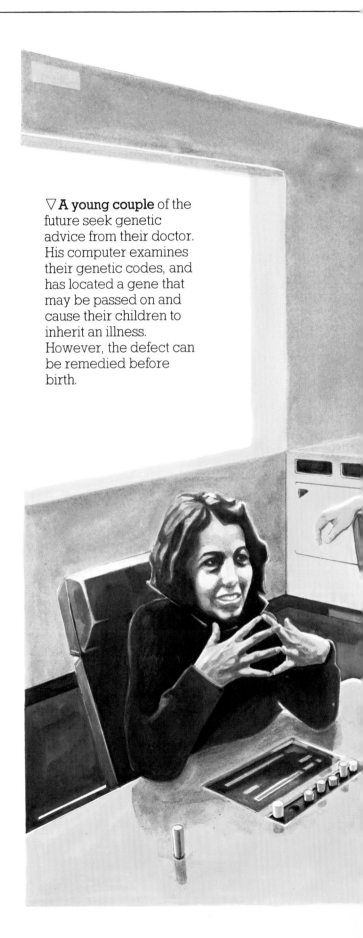

▽ **A young couple** of the future seek genetic advice from their doctor. His computer examines their genetic codes, and has located a gene that may be passed on and cause their children to inherit an illness. However, the defect can be remedied before birth.

Medicine before birth

In the world of tomorrow doctors will be able to watch over people and care for them from the very moment that life begins. This is not the time of birth but the point at which the future baby begins to grow as an embryo inside its mother. By the time the baby is born, it will if necessary have received months of medical attention.

Already doctors can inspect an unborn child with detectors using ultrasonic sound waves that bounce harmlessly off the baby in the mother's womb. They can also take fluid from the womb and check it to make sure that all is going well with the baby as it grows. In the future these techniques should develop so that it will be possible to see both the inside and outside of the unborn baby's body. Doctors will be able to watch over its development as easily as if the baby were already born.

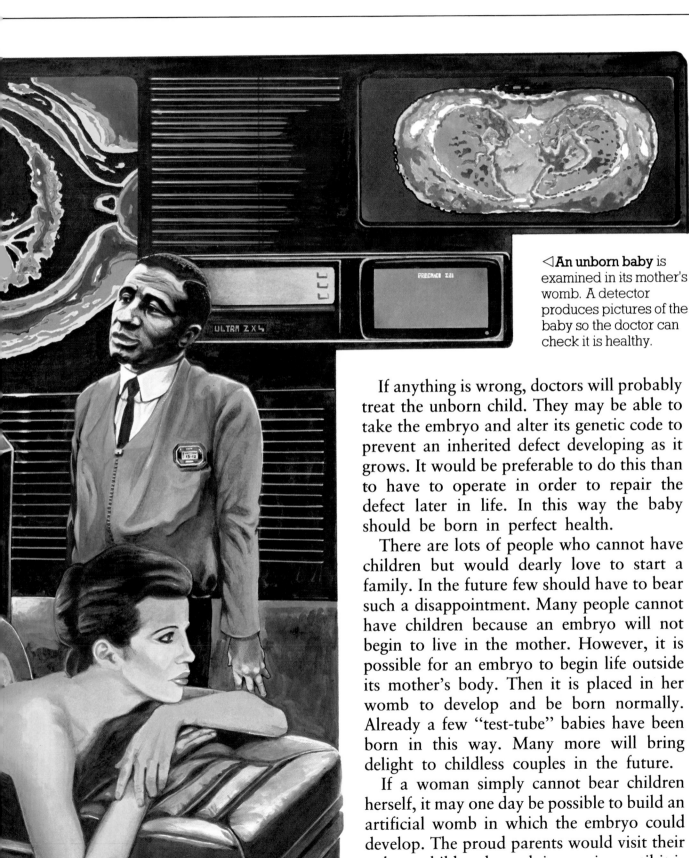

◁ **An unborn baby** is examined in its mother's womb. A detector produces pictures of the baby so the doctor can check it is healthy.

If anything is wrong, doctors will probably treat the unborn child. They may be able to take the embryo and alter its genetic code to prevent an inherited defect developing as it grows. It would be preferable to do this than to have to operate in order to repair the defect later in life. In this way the baby should be born in perfect health.

There are lots of people who cannot have children but would dearly love to start a family. In the future few should have to bear such a disappointment. Many people cannot have children because an embryo will not begin to live in the mother. However, it is possible for an embryo to begin life outside its mother's body. Then it is placed in her womb to develop and be born normally. Already a few "test-tube" babies have been born in this way. Many more will bring delight to childless couples in the future.

If a woman simply cannot bear children herself, it may one day be possible to build an artificial womb in which the embryo could develop. The proud parents would visit their unborn child and watch it growing until it is ready to be born, when it would simply be lifted out!

13

Helping yourself

By checking the genetic codes of parents and by caring for unborn babies, the children of tomorrow should be born in perfect health. A long life is likely to lie ahead of them. But to remain healthy, everyone will have to look after themselves. As now, this will mean taking exercise, keeping clean and behaving sensibly to avoid danger. However, the world of tomorrow will bring other ways in which you can help to prevent yourself from getting ill.

Many people fall ill because they have an allergy. Something they eat or drink disagrees with them, or perhaps something in the air upsets them. Tiny particles of pollen blown by the wind give some people hay fever, for example. Others cannot eat food made from flour or shellfish without feeling ill. Often these people suffer for years before they find out what is wrong.

▽ **Young people** test themselves at a health complex of the future. One girl works a machine that plays games needing quick and accurate movements. In this way, it tests her ability to respond to situations. The boy is testing his eyesight, while the other girl faces a machine that examines her hand. A doctor is present to advise the children.

In the future you will be able to go to the doctor or a health complex to prepare yourself for a healthy life. Machines will take samples such as blood, saliva, hair and body wastes. They will measure them to find out exactly how your body reacts to food and drink and to substances in air and water. Then a computer will take the measurements and work out which things are likely to cause problems for you. It will produce a personal list of things to do and to avoid if you want to stay healthy and feel alert and full of energy. It is certain, for example, to insist that you should never smoke. It may even recommend certain rules for making the best of your memory and intelligence. Following a list of rules might seem to make life a lot less fun. However, it would probably be no more trouble than taking care when crossing the road, for example.

Tooth troubles

A visit to the dentist in the future will no longer hold the fears that it has for lots of people today. Even though painkillers make dentistry painless, receiving injections and having your teeth drilled is unpleasant to many people. However, the dentist should not have to wield either a needle or a drill in your mouth for very much longer.

A dentist uses a drill to grind decay out of a tooth. Soon it should be possible to treat tooth decay with a liquid that dissolves the decayed part of the tooth. The dentist will simply spray it on your teeth instead of using a drill. Then you'll wash away the decay by rinsing your mouth out with some water before the dentist fills the hole left in the tooth.

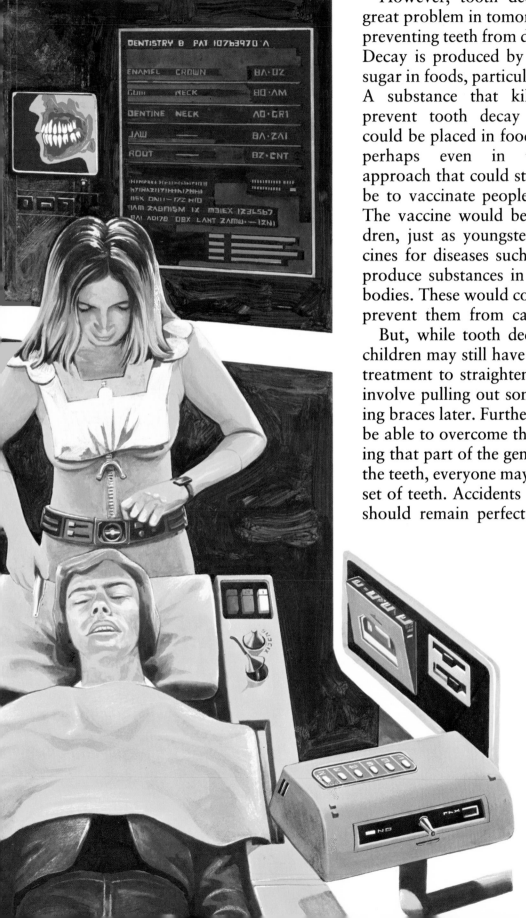

However, tooth decay should not be a great problem in tomorrow's world. Ways of preventing teeth from decaying will be found. Decay is produced by bacteria that feed on sugar in foods, particularly sweets or candies. A substance that kills the bacteria will prevent tooth decay from developing. It could be placed in food, in a mouthwash, or perhaps even in toothpaste. Another approach that could stop the bacteria would be to vaccinate people against tooth decay. The vaccine would be given to young children, just as youngsters can now take vaccines for diseases such as measles. It would produce substances in the body called antibodies. These would combat the bacteria and prevent them from causing tooth decay.

But, while tooth decay should disappear, children may still have to visit the dentist for treatment to straighten their teeth. This can involve pulling out some first teeth or wearing braces later. Further in the future we may be able to overcome this problem. By changing that part of the genetic code that governs the teeth, everyone may be born with an ideal set of teeth. Accidents apart, this set of teeth should remain perfect for life.

◁ **A dentist** of the future examines the teeth of a young patient. She holds a mouth scanner which produces an image of the interior of the teeth on a screen. The dentist can see right away if the teeth need any attention. There is no drill to treat any decay that the patient may have. Instead, the dentist uses a liquid that simply removes decay from the teeth before filling them.

Computer doctor

A visit to the doctor in the future is likely to resemble a computer game, for computers will be greatly involved in medical care. Now doctors have to question and examine their patients to find out what is wrong with them. They compare the patients' answers and the examination results with their own knowledge of medical conditions and illnesses. This enables doctors to decide on the causes of the patients' problems.

Computers can store huge amounts of medical information. Doctors are therefore likely to use computers to help them find the causes of illnesses. The computer could take over completely, allowing doctors to concentrate on patients who need personal care.

▽ **Patients** visiting a doctor in the future first tell the doctor's computer what is wrong with them. The computer may provide a remedy, or tell the patient to go to the next sections to be tested or to give samples. The doctor sees patients who need personal attention.

The computer will question the patient about an illness just as the doctor does now. It will either display words on a screen or speak to the patient, who will reply or operate a keyboard to answer. The questions will continue until the computer has either narrowed down the possible causes of the illness to one or needs more information that the patient cannot give by answering.

The patient will then go to a machine that checks his or her physical condition. It will measure such factors as pulse, temperature and blood pressure and maybe look into the interior of the patient's body. The results will go to the computer. This may still not provide the computer with enough information about the patient, and it may need to take samples — for example, of blood or hair. It will do this painlessly. Finally, the computer will dispense drugs and prescribe treatment, but a doctor will be present to discuss its results if the patient wishes.

The war against disease

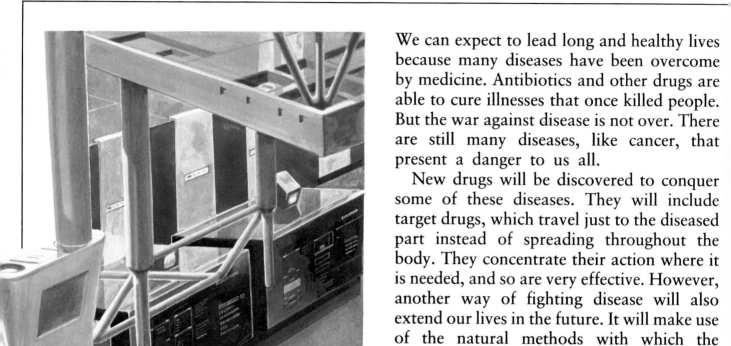

We can expect to lead long and healthy lives because many diseases have been overcome by medicine. Antibiotics and other drugs are able to cure illnesses that once killed people. But the war against disease is not over. There are still many diseases, like cancer, that present a danger to us all.

New drugs will be discovered to conquer some of these diseases. They will include target drugs, which travel just to the diseased part instead of spreading throughout the body. They concentrate their action where it is needed, and so are very effective. However, another way of fighting disease will also extend our lives in the future. It will make use of the natural methods with which the human body defends itself against invading bacteria and viruses.

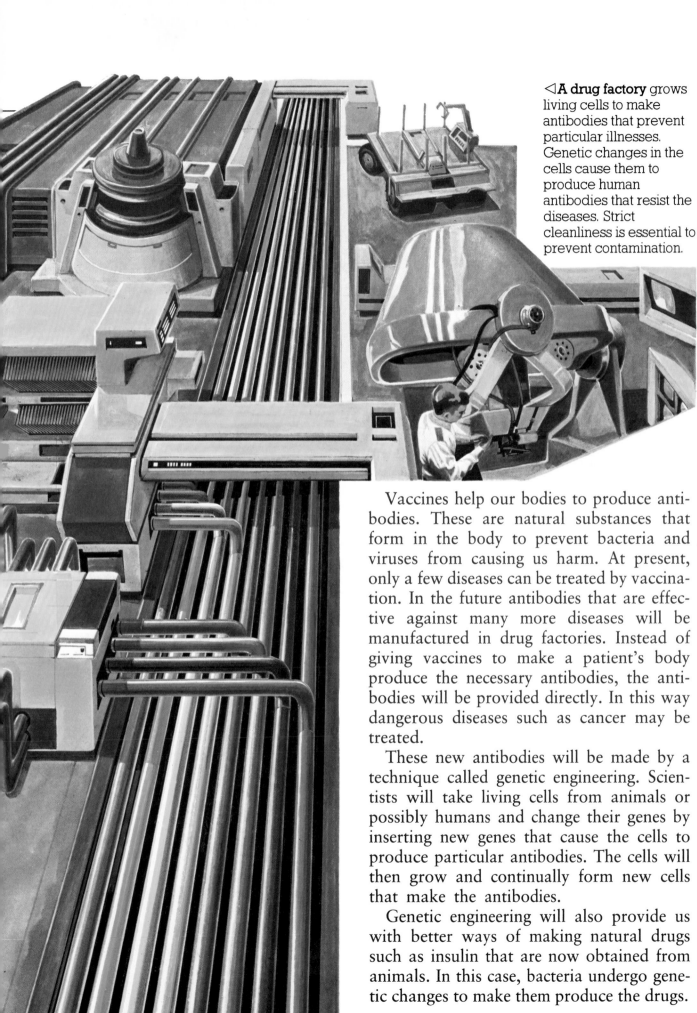

◁ **A drug factory** grows living cells to make antibodies that prevent particular illnesses. Genetic changes in the cells cause them to produce human antibodies that resist the diseases. Strict cleanliness is essential to prevent contamination.

Vaccines help our bodies to produce antibodies. These are natural substances that form in the body to prevent bacteria and viruses from causing us harm. At present, only a few diseases can be treated by vaccination. In the future antibodies that are effective against many more diseases will be manufactured in drug factories. Instead of giving vaccines to make a patient's body produce the necessary antibodies, the antibodies will be provided directly. In this way dangerous diseases such as cancer may be treated.

These new antibodies will be made by a technique called genetic engineering. Scientists will take living cells from animals or possibly humans and change their genes by inserting new genes that cause the cells to produce particular antibodies. The cells will then grow and continually form new cells that make the antibodies.

Genetic engineering will also provide us with better ways of making natural drugs such as insulin that are now obtained from animals. In this case, bacteria undergo genetic changes to make them produce the drugs.

21

Exploring the body

Imagine being able to look inside a living person and see how their heart, brain and all their other organs are working. This is the exciting prospect that the future holds for doctors. Machines called scanners are allowing doctors and surgeons to look into living human bodies without cutting them open. Unlike X-ray photographs, which give only outlines of bones and internal organs, scanners produce pictures showing them in great detail. Some provide moving pictures, so that doctors can see how living organs are behaving.

This means that the doctors of the future will be able to see immediately and exactly what is wrong with a patient and take action right away. The scanners will also be invaluable in checking people to prevent disorders building up. Doctors will be able to look into your heart and lungs to make sure they are working properly and inspect your veins and arteries to check that your blood is flowing easily around your body. They will see into your brain and make certain that nothing is affecting your mental health.

The doctors will not only use scanners to find out what is wrong with people. They will also be able to follow treatment, for example with drugs, to see that it is working properly. Research scientists will also find scanners essential to their work in understanding exactly how the human body operates. Scanners can depict parts inside the body in great detail. They could, for example, reveal how the stomach digests food to find out why some people are fat and others are thin.

Most scanners work by firing harmless beams of ultrasound or radio waves into the body. The various layers of tissue inside the body reflect ultrasound, and detectors build up a picture from the reflected sound waves. Radio waves pass through the body, but are affected by the tissues, enabling receivers to form a picture of the interior.

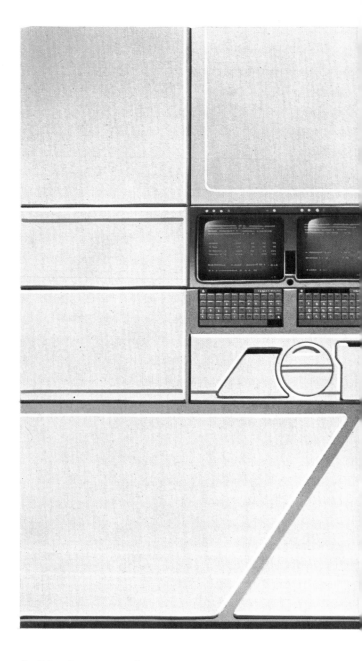

▷ **A body scanner** is ready to receive a patient. Inside the scanner, harmless beams penetrate the patient's body. The scanner detects the beams that emerge and uses them to produce detailed pictures of the interior of the patient's body. In this way the doctors can see what is causing the patient's illness.

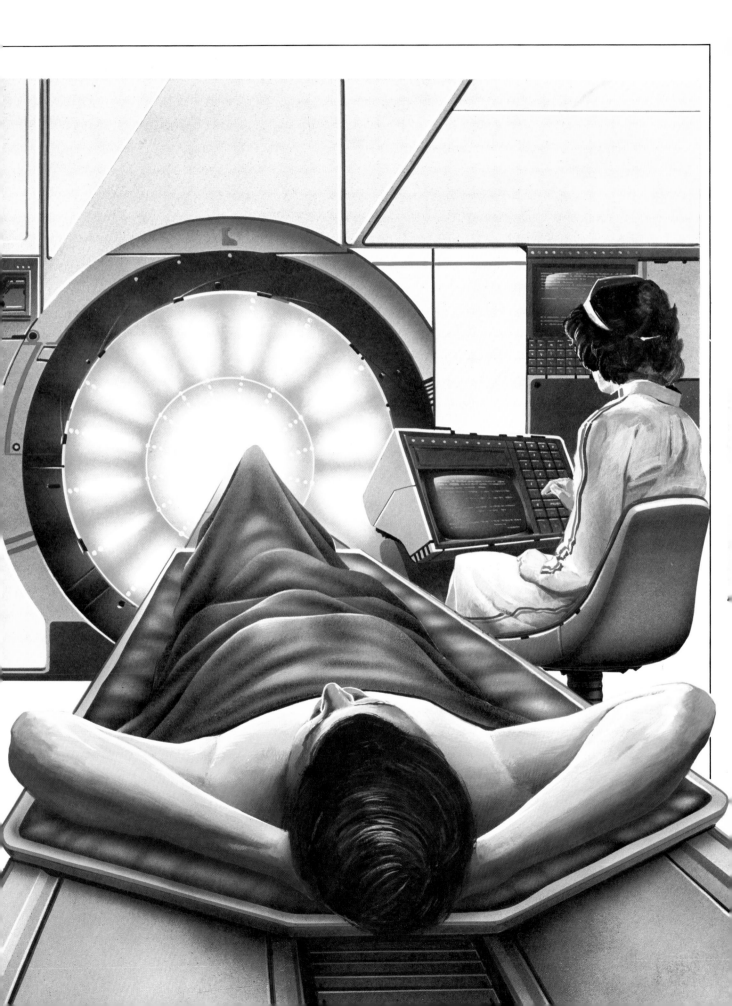

Emergency room

Improved medical care will make the world of tomorrow a healthier world for us all. However, it will not make the world a safer place to live in. People are still going to have accidents and suffer violence, and the emergency room of the hospital of the future will be constantly busy with casualties. But with new kinds of treatment, many more victims of severe accidents and violence will recover and survive.

Poisoning is a common accident, especially among young children who swallow drugs thinking they are sweets or candies. Poison victims will be rushed to the emergency room, and a computer will analyze the drugs or the person's blood to identify the poison immediately. Machines will then remove the poison from the patient's body in minutes.

Burns are among the most serious accidents. The heat of a severe burn destroys the skin, and people with large and severe burns are now likely to die. However, special kinds of artificial skin will save more and more burn victims. This skin is applied to the burned area and protects the patient while new skin grows beneath it. The artificial skin is then peeled away.

The emergency room will also have to deal with people who have been shot or stabbed and people who are near death from drowning. Emergency operations will repair any damage to the body, but these patients may suffer brain damage as well. This is not because the brain is physically harmed but because the supply of blood to the brain falls. The brain is then damaged in minutes, causing paralysis and possibly death. However, the future should bring ways of delaying brain damage in casualties. New drugs may keep the brain from deteriorating while the patient undergoes emergency treatment. Finding a way to keep the brain alive in emergencies will be one of the most important advances in medicine. Once this is achieved, many people will be saved from death or terrible disability.

◁ **Ambulance attendants** rush accident victims into the emergency entrance of a hospital of the future. Behind, helicopters bring in more casualties needing emergency treatment.

Hospital of the future

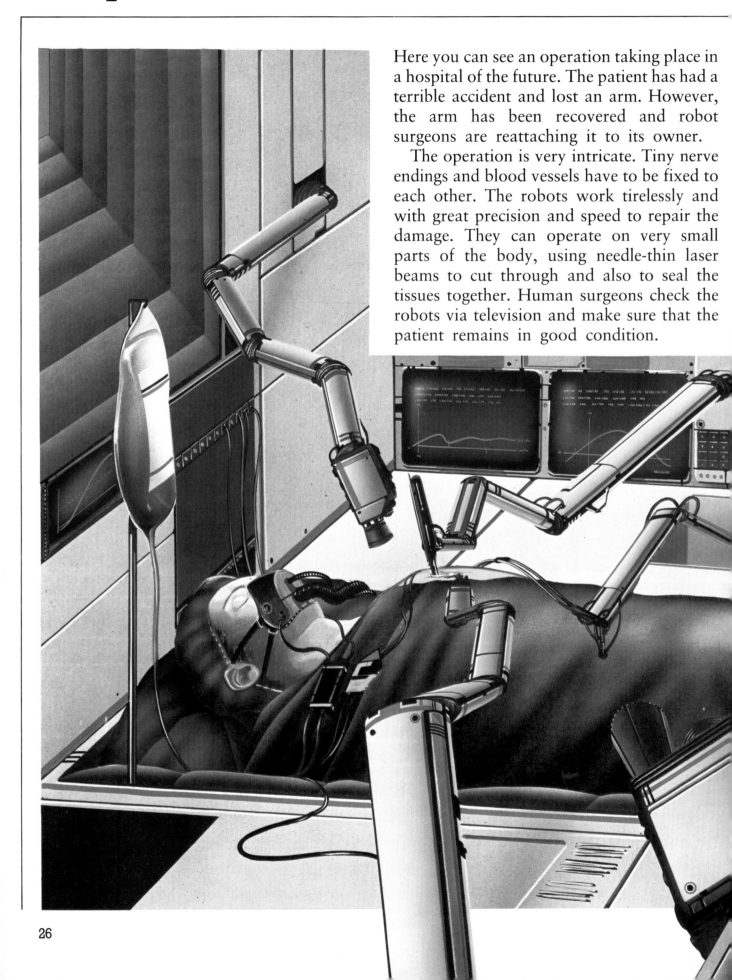

Here you can see an operation taking place in a hospital of the future. The patient has had a terrible accident and lost an arm. However, the arm has been recovered and robot surgeons are reattaching it to its owner.

The operation is very intricate. Tiny nerve endings and blood vessels have to be fixed to each other. The robots work tirelessly and with great precision and speed to repair the damage. They can operate on very small parts of the body, using needle-thin laser beams to cut through and also to seal the tissues together. Human surgeons check the robots via television and make sure that the patient remains in good condition.

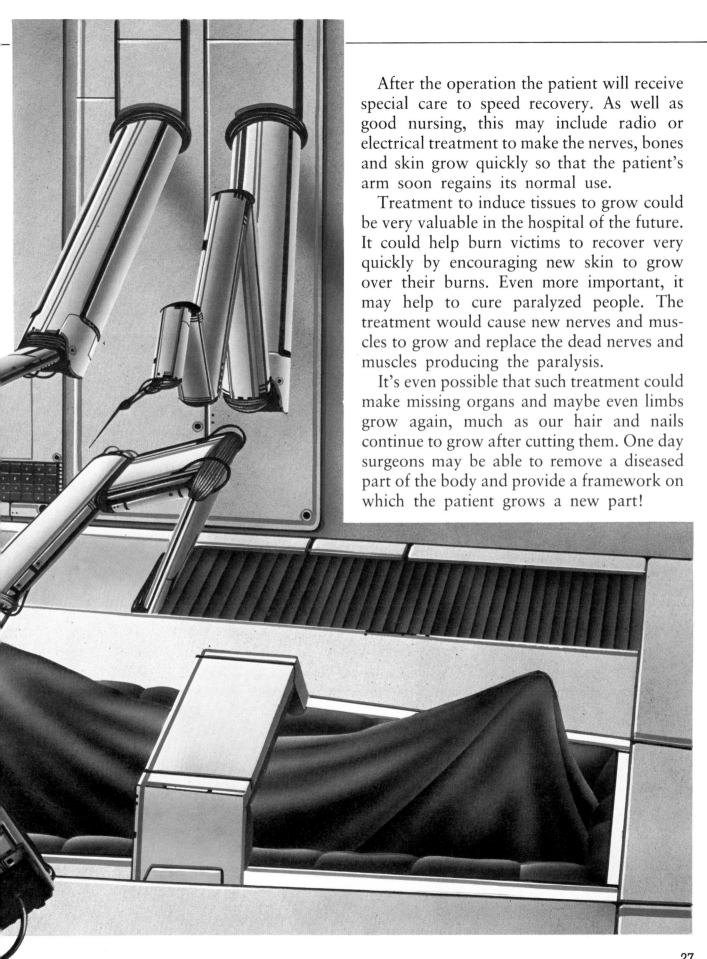

After the operation the patient will receive special care to speed recovery. As well as good nursing, this may include radio or electrical treatment to make the nerves, bones and skin grow quickly so that the patient's arm soon regains its normal use.

Treatment to induce tissues to grow could be very valuable in the hospital of the future. It could help burn victims to recover very quickly by encouraging new skin to grow over their burns. Even more important, it may help to cure paralyzed people. The treatment would cause new nerves and muscles to grow and replace the dead nerves and muscles producing the paralysis.

It's even possible that such treatment could make missing organs and maybe even limbs grow again, much as our hair and nails continue to grow after cutting them. One day surgeons may be able to remove a diseased part of the body and provide a framework on which the patient grows a new part!

Spare-part medicine

In the future, no one should have to fear the failure or loss of any part of their body — either through disease or by accident. Hospitals should have banks of organs that will replace any defective or missing part. Already many people have been given a new life by receiving replacement kidneys. Others are living with new hearts beating inside their chests. In tomorrow's world it should also be possible for surgeons to transplant other parts of the body — a stomach, lung or liver and maybe even another hand, foot, arm or leg!

Most spare parts will come, as most do today, from dead people. Because delay causes damage, the organs have to be placed in their new owners shortly after the death of the donors. Often there is not enough time to get a part to a patient in need of it. There's another problem too. The body tissues of the patient must match the tissue of the new organ if it is to continue working. Otherwise the body will reject the organ and it will cease to function.

These problems should be overcome in the future. Ways of preserving spare organs should be found, perhaps by cooling them and treating them with drugs. Scanners will be able to look inside the organs and check that they are not damaged. Computers will help to match the tissues of patients with the spare parts, but rejection may also be conquered by new drugs.

Another important transplant technique is to place new bone marrow in people to fight blood cancer. The bone marrow can be taken from living people without harming them, but it has to match the patient. If this proves difficult, doctors may be able to treat this cancer and some other diseases by taking blood cells from young people and preserving them. If they later develop the diseases, the patients could have injections of their own preserved healthy blood to cure them!

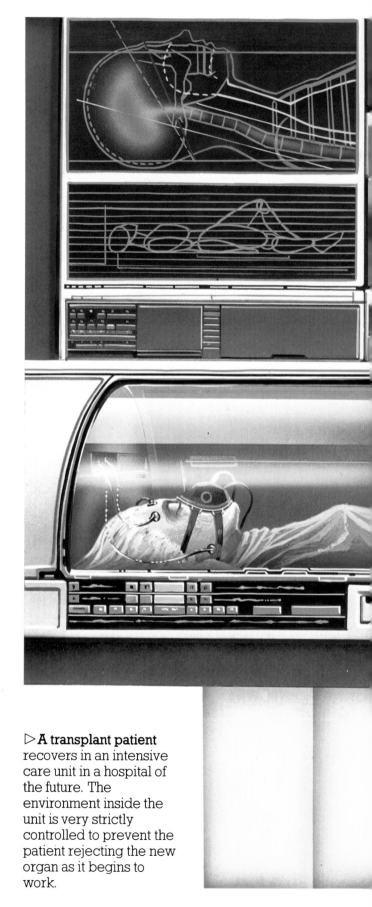

▷ **A transplant patient** recovers in an intensive care unit in a hospital of the future. The environment inside the unit is very strictly controlled to prevent the patient rejecting the new organ as it begins to work.

Bionic people

Replacing organs with transplants is only one way of helping people who lose the use of parts of their body. Artificial organs can be inserted instead. In the future many people may survive accidents or disease by becoming part human and part machine. The bionic man or woman could become a reality.

Already, of course, people who lose an arm or leg can be fitted with an artificial limb. However, the new arm or leg is limited in the movements it can perform. In tomorrow's world artificial limbs will work as well as real ones or perhaps even better. Inside the limbs, tiny computers will control miniature motors to work like real muscles. The motors will drive artificial elbows, knees, wrists, ankles, fingers and toes to carry out all the complicated movements we use in our everyday lives. The computers will be linked to the nerves that normally carry impulses from our brains to our muscles.

This means that the person will only have to think of a movement and the artificial limb will perform it. Electronic sensors in its artificial skin will enable the user to feel what the limb is doing and so provide the sensation of touch.

People may also be fitted with other artificial organs, such as mechanical hearts or kidneys. Electronic nerves may replace dead nerves, enabling paralyzed people to move again. Does this mean that people could be given mechanical parts that would enable them to run faster and beat normal people at everything? And could we continually replace worn and faulty organs and live for ever?

An artificial organ could be made very powerful. However, it's doubtful that the rest of the body would stand the strain it would produce. To prevent aging, parts of the brain would have to be replaced as well as faulty organs. This may be possible one day, but replacement of the brain would produce a new person with different thoughts.

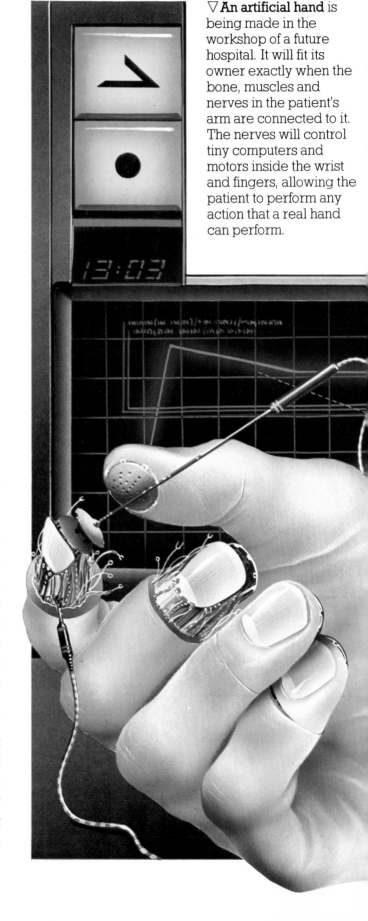

▽ **An artificial hand** is being made in the workshop of a future hospital. It will fit its owner exactly when the bone, muscles and nerves in the patient's arm are connected to it. The nerves will control tiny computers and motors inside the wrist and fingers, allowing the patient to perform any action that a real hand can perform.

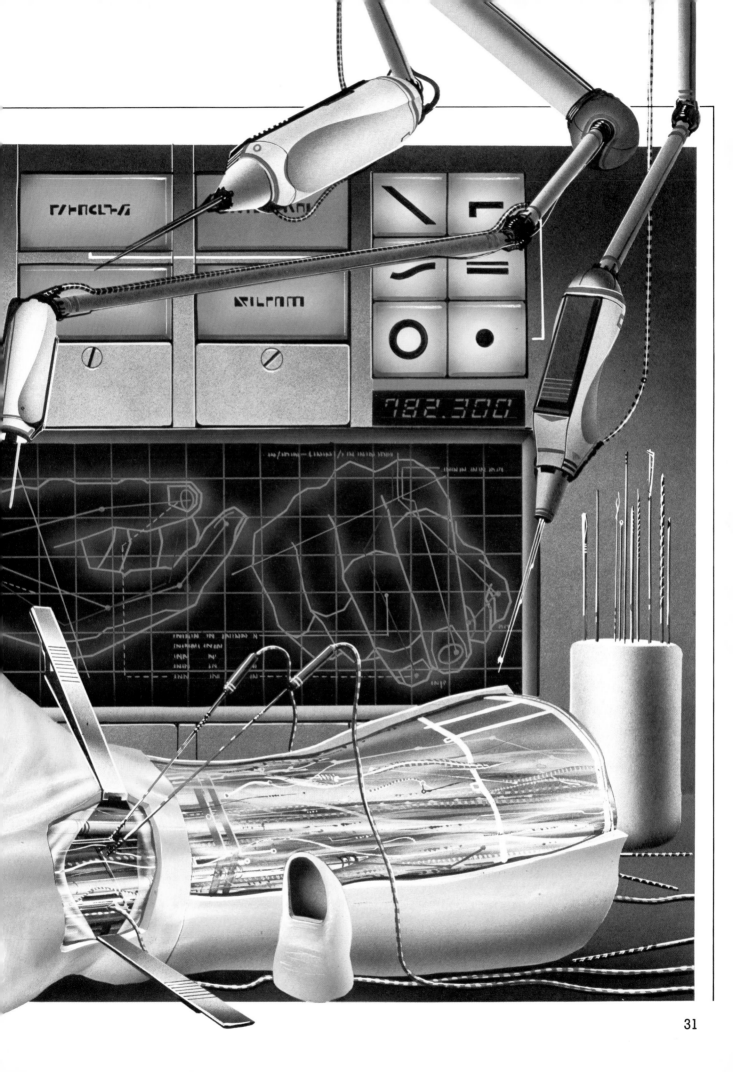

Aiding the disabled

No one need fear being disabled in to-morrow's world. Transplants or artificial organs should be able to restore the power of movement so that the wheelchair will become obsolete. Furthermore, similar techniques should enable the blind to see, the deaf to hear and the mute or dumb to speak.

Blind people are likely to see again or for the first time with tiny television cameras for eyes. The cameras could be implanted into the person's eyes. Signals from the cameras would go to the visual part of the brain that "sees" images. This would copy the way in which signals from real eyes go along the optic nerves to the brain. In similar ways, deaf people could hear with electronic aids implanted in their ears and connected to the brain. Mute people could talk with electronic devices that "speak" when fed with speech signals from the brain.

▷ **A blind boy** and his father visit an eye doctor in the future. The doctor is explaining that he will see when the two tiny eye-like cameras are fitted. These artificial eyes will produce signals that will go to the boy's brain to make him see. Images produced by the eyes are showing on the two video screens.

However, these developments probably lie some way in the future. In the meantime, technology rather than medicine will aid the disabled. Computers will soon be able to respond fully to spoken commands. Disabled people in wheelchairs will only need to speak to computerized machines or robots to get help at any time.

Computers will also be able to talk as well as listen. They will be able to read to blind people from books and letters, and mute people will be able to instruct computers to utter sentences for them. Computers will also come to the aid of the deaf. Machines will be able to listen to speech and display the words on a screen, allowing deaf people to understand others. Many deaf people cannot speak because they cannot hear, and computers will be able to train them to make the correct sounds and talk.

Conquering pain

No matter how healthy we may be, one very important future development in medicine is going to affect us all. We all feel pain at times, while some unlucky people spend much of their lives in pain. However, in the world of tomorrow new painkillers should ensure that no one need ever suffer pain. No longer will headaches, stomachaches or the pains of injuries or diseases blight our lives.

We have painkillers now of course, ranging from mild remedies like aspirin to powerful drugs such as morphine. However, these medicines are harmful in large quantities. They cannot prevent agonizing pain without poisoning the patient or producing serious side effects like drug addiction. The painkillers of the future will not cause harm to the people taking them and yet should stop even the most searing pain. This is because they will employ the body's natural methods of fighting pain.

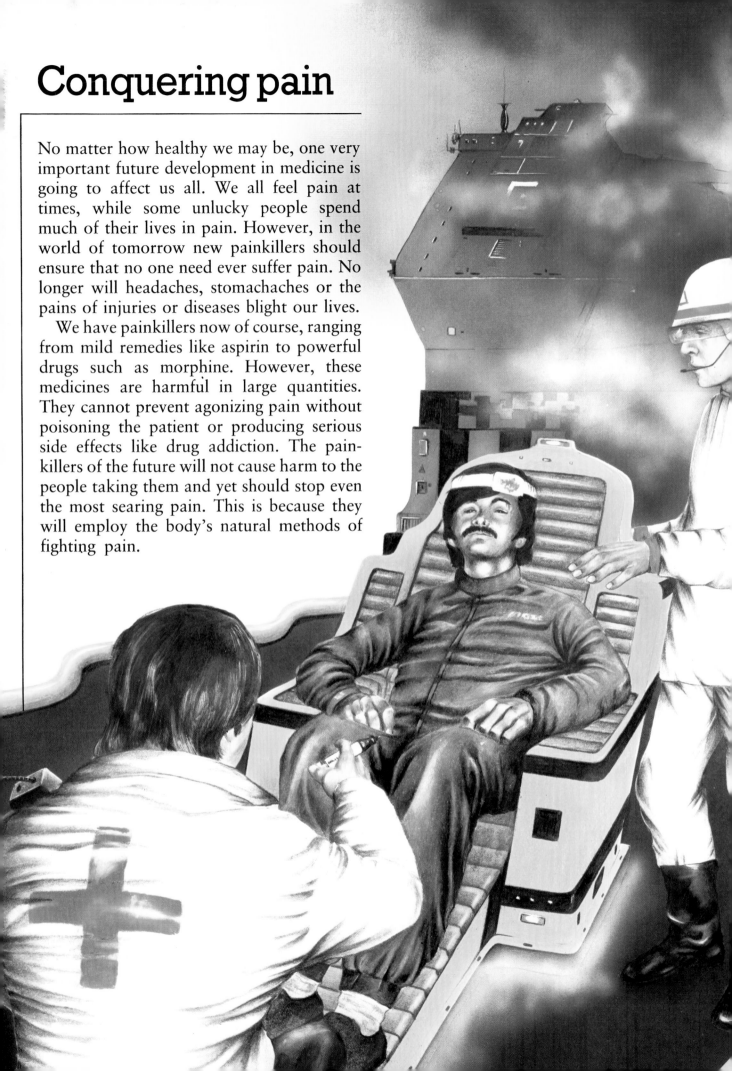

It may seem odd to say that we have our own ways of killing pain. They don't seem to work if we burn ourselves, for example. However, the pain of a small injury makes us move away from its cause, preventing further harm. Serious injuries can be different and people who are badly injured often do not feel any pain right away. The injury makes their bodies produce natural painkilling substances and these act on the nerves or brain to suppress all pain. With acupuncture, pain can be prevented by sticking needles into the body, possibly because natural painkillers are produced. Applying low electric currents may also stop pain for the same reason.

In the near future techniques like genetic engineering should enable chemists to produce these natural painkillers, probably in the form of pills. It seems likely that they will be far more powerful than today's most effective drugs. Furthermore they should not harm the body in any way. With natural painkillers available everywhere, the future should be free of pain for everyone.

◁ **A fire** has broken out and doctors rush to the scene to treat people with severe burns. A man who has been injured in the fire is being taken to an ambulance. He feels no pain, even though burns are normally agonizing. A doctor has given him natural painkillers, which remove all pain and allow him to relax.

Glossary

Antibiotic
A drug which kills bacteria and some other germs or micro-organisms that cause disease. Antibiotics are produced by growing certain other bacteria or micro-organisms. They are also made from chemicals. Penicillin is an antibiotic.

Antibody
A substance that forms naturally in the body to combat a particular foreign body or infection. Antibodies may remain in the body and prevent the infection occurring again.

Bacteria
Tiny living things that may cause disease. Some bacteria invade the body and produce poisons that make us ill. However, many other bacteria live in the body without causing any harm. Some bacteria help it to work.

Bone marrow
The soft substance in the middle of bones. Red blood cells are formed in bone marrow.

Cancer
A disease in which a part of the body begins to grow in an abnormal way, often preventing it from working properly. Cancer has many causes.

Cell
The human body is made up of millions of tiny living cells that work together to keep the body alive. There are many different kinds of cells, such as blood cells and bone cells. Animals and plants also consist of cells. An egg is a large cell, for example.

Drug addiction
A condition in which the withdrawal of a drug produces unpleasant effects on a person. Drug addicts therefore cannot stop taking a drug, even though it may be harmful to them.

Embryo
An unborn baby in the first stage of development in its mother's womb. It is an embryo for about two months, after which the baby begins to look human.

Genes
All living cells contain genes, which are made up of certain combinations of chemicals. Every cell in a living thing has the same individual set of genes with their own particular chemical combinations. These genes determine all the characteristics of the living thing and make it different from all other living things.

Genetic code
The arrangement of chemicals within a gene.

Nerves
Long threads that run through the body from the brain and backbone to all the organs in the body. The nerves carry electrical signals that operate the organs. They produce intentional movements, such as raising an arm, as well as automatic operations, such as breathing. Nerves also carry sensations of touch and pain to the brain.

Organ
Any separate part of the body that works in its own particular way. For example, the brain, heart, liver and eyes are all organs.

Paralysis
A condition in which a person is unable to make his or her muscles work, and so cannot move either a part of the body or possibly the whole body.

Patient
Anyone who is getting medical care or treatment.

Scanner
A machine that can produce a picture of the inside of the body or an organ.

Tissues
The different kinds of materials that make up the body. They include muscle tissue, skin tissue, bone tissue and so on.

Transplant
An organ that is taken from one person and placed inside another person to replace a defective organ, such as a kidney.

Ultrasound
Sound that is so high in pitch that it cannot be heard.

Vaccine
A preparation containing bacteria or viruses that is given to people to make them produce antibodies, and so prevent them getting a particular disease.

Virus
A tiny living thing that can invade a cell and harm the cell so it causes disease.

X-rays
Invisible rays that can penetrate flesh but not bone. X-ray pictures of the body show up bones and also the outlines of various organs.

ndex

:ident 24–5
ipuncture 35
ergy 14
ibiotic 20, 36
ibody 17, 21, 36
.ficial eye 32–3
.ficial limb 30–1
.ficial skin 25, 30

:teria 17, 20–1, 36
nics 30–1
.dness 32–3
od 15, 19, 22, 28
ie marrow 28, 36
.in 22, 25, 30, 32, 35
rn 25, 27, 35

icer 21, 28, 36
l 21, 36
nputer 10, 15, 18–19,
8, 30, 33

afness 32–3
ntistry 16–17
.abled people 32–3
nor 28
ig 19, 20–1, 25, 34
ig addiction 34, 36

embryo 12–13, 36

gene 10, 21, 36
genetic code 10, 13, 17,
  36
genetic engineering 21,
  35

health complex 14–15
hospital 24–9

intelligence 15

laser 26

memory 15
mental health 10, 22
muscle 27, 30

nerve 27, 30, 35, 36

operation 26–7

painkiller 34–5
paralysis 25, 27, 30, 36
poison 24

robot 26, 33

scanner 22–3, 28, 36

teeth 16–17
test-tube baby 13
tissue 22, 27, 28, 36
transplant 28–9, 32, 36

ultrasound 12, 22, 36

vaccine 17, 21, 36
virus 20–1, 36

X-rays 22, 36

Designed by Aladdin Books Ltd
70 Old Compton Street, London W1

Art Editor
Ben White

Designer   *Typography*
David West   Malcolm Smythe

Illustrators
Richard Dunn   Peter Holt
Andrew Farmer   Tom Stimpson
Chris Forsey

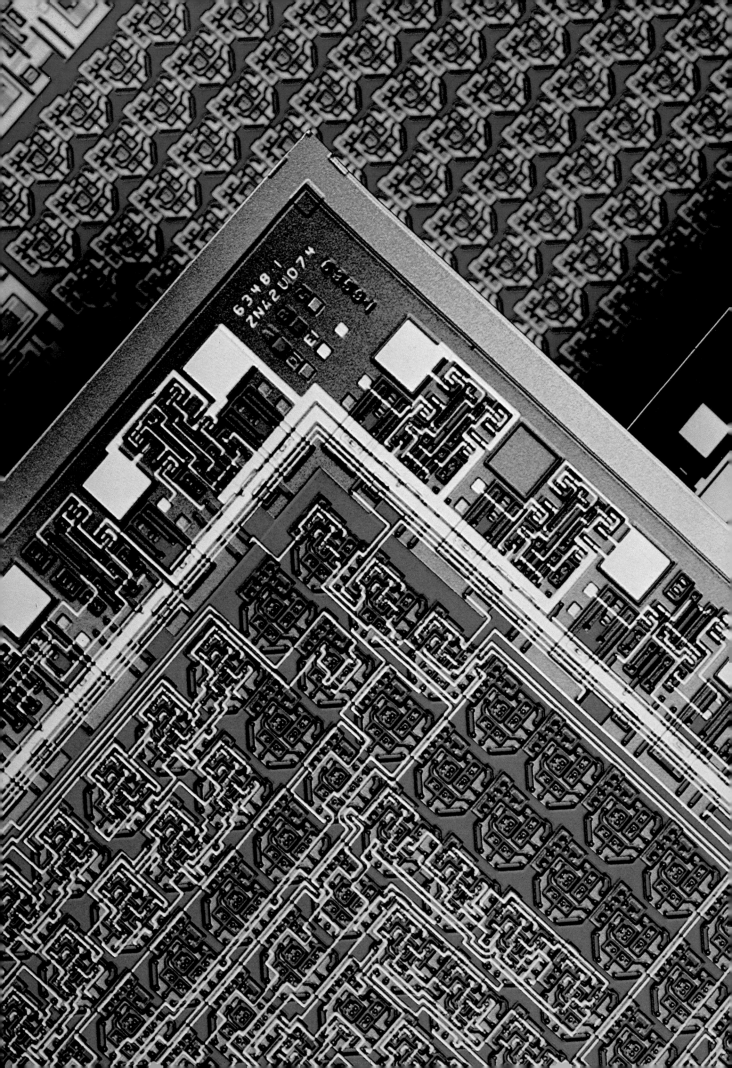